As if Gravity Were a Theory

Poems by
Don Colburn

Winner of the 2005 Cider Press Review Book Award

Cider Press Review
Halifax, PA

Printed in Austin, TX by Morgan Printing.

Author photograph taken by Motoya Nakamura.

Cover assembled by Caron Andregg.

The text of this book is composed in Garamond.

First Edition

1 2 3 4 5 6 7 8 9 0

ISBN 1-930781-01-6

Published by

Cider Press Review
777 Braddock Lane
Halifax, PA 17032

For additional information visit **ciderpressreview.com**.

For my teachers
especially my first and best coach
Bob Colburn
and years later in another field
Simone Di Piero

Contents

III

Acknowledgements:

Grateful acknowledgement goes to the magazines where many of these poems first appeared, sometimes in different form:

Alaska Quarterly Review ("The Wish" and "Touchstones")
Annals of Internal Medicine ("Sunday Morning, Long-term Care Wing")
Antietam Review ("Motel, East Ohio" and "The Farmer")
Cider Press Review ("Sestina Insomnia" and "Only Life")
Cimarron Review ("Wrecking Ball")
Circumference ("Veterans Day Night at the War Memorial" and "What I Didn't Tell Stephen")
The Comstock Review ("The Moose")
Explorations ("Why Sarah Will Never Suffer Writer's Block")
Hedge Apple ("Toward the End of the Year")
The Iowa Review ("In the Workshop After I Read My Poem Aloud," "Fall Migration at Brigantine," "To Bill Buckner on his Release by the Red Sox," "Etheridge" and "Emerson and I Stare at the Sunset")
The Journal ("Storm on Lopez Island")
Kansas Quarterly ("To the Computer Who Lost to a Human at Chess")
Lullwater Review ("Last Day of Summer, 1954")
Margie ("The Telling" and "Edward Dickinson, Emily's Dad")
The Madison Review ("Martins Ferry," "Late" and "4 Orange")
The Nation ("Wildflowers")
Plainsongs ("Local News," "Days" and "Timberline")
Ploughshares ("There," "To a Condemned Man Now Dead" and "On the Eighteenth Day of Bombing, I Go for a Hike")
Poet Lore ("De Kooning in Court at Eighty-five," "To Lee Atwater on his Fortieth Birthday" and "Pansies at the Modern")
Poetry Northwest ("Prayer")
Prairie Schooner ("Birds," "Differences" and "Cul-de-sac")
Virginia Quarterly Review ("Given" and "The Luxury of Distance")

Warren Wilson Review ("The Art of Poetry")
Wilderness ("Elegy in March" and "Morning Song")
Zone 3 ("At Kennedy & Georgia," "As if Gravity Were a Theory" and "The Hill")

Special thanks to The MacDowell Colony and Centrum Foundation.

"In the Workshop After I Read My Poem Aloud" was reprinted in *Hard Choices: An Iowa Review Reader*, edited by David Hamilton (University of Iowa Press: 1996); *In the Palm of Your Hand: The Poet's Portable Workshop*, by Steve Kowit (Tilbury House: 1995); *The Portable Poetry Workshop*, by Jack Myers (Wadsworth: 2005), and *The Starving Artist's Survival Guide,* by Marianne Taylor and Laurie Lindop (Simon Spotlight Entertainment: 2005).

"Fall Migration at Brigantine" was reprinted in *Hungry As We Are: An Anthology of Washington Area Poets,* edited by Ann Darr (Washington Writers' Publishing House: 1995), and *Under A Gull's Wing: Poems and Photographs of the Jersey Shore,* edited by Rich Youmans and Frank Finale (Down the Shore Publishing: 1996).

"Morning Song" was reprinted in *Wild Song: Poems of the Natural World*, edited by John Daniel (University of Georgia Press: 1998).

"Wildflowers" was reprinted in *Cabin Fever: Poets at Joaquin Miller's Cabin, 1984-2001*, edited by Jacklyn W. Potter, Dwaine Rieves and Gary Stein (Word Works: 2003).

Some of these poems appeared in the chapbook *Another Way to Begin* (Finishing Line Press: 2006).

Foreword

Often these days I am asked to judge a few poetry contests which I do with great pleasure because reading manuscripts helps me stay in tune with the new voices, and by extension the new voices help me stay feeling young and connected. It is never easy to read through a long list of final manuscripts and then pick a winner (a word I'm not too crazy about) but the task, though often daunting and time consuming, is still quite pleasurable to me because I read with both an open mind and an open heart, not necessarily looking for a "winner" (I'm not sure I know what one wins in the larger scheme of things), but for the one manuscript with which I keep dialogue. A manuscript that immediately begins to lure me to its pages, its words, its voice . . .

This is clearly the case with what happened with Don Colburn's book of poems, *As if Gravity Were a Theory.* I began by succumbing to the book's title, its wide-eyed assertions and possibilities, and then to its pages filled with energized poems . . . poem after poem, I fell into this book's charm and the thought-provoking landscape of so many of the poems. Mr. Colburn, one comes to realize rather quickly as one begins to enjoy the book, is not only a master craftsperson, but one possessed of the gift of story-telling. To say these poems are lucid and gem-like is an understatement: They are that and more.

The book is smartly separated into three parts, not equal in the number of pages or poems, but each building on the last, washing over the reader like a succession of mounting waves. The last part is the longest and the most affecting; here the poems fall upon you like a strong tropical downpour. You, reader, are invited to read on after "Given," "Elegy in March," and "Storm on Lopez Island," because you quickly become very aware that this is a fresh new voice, someone who can handle the nuances of language with grace, and dare I say, *beauty*.

By the time I reached "Wrecking Ball," I was in essence mesmerized by the poet's command, and by the fact that here is a poet not afraid to use trouble-maker words like "beauty." And he does so with great effect.

I believe this is one of those rare cases of a poet madly in love with the world, clearly, the way good poets always are. Early parts of this book display a great variety in terms of form and content. There's an organic rhythm being relayed to us, and certainly by the time you arrive at the title poem in this book you are won over: "...Snow is falling everywhere, even/ up from the tarmac in the trembling / around the engine barrels. / . . . No cottonwoods to give the river away, no river. / No earth, no edge. Not one fact / to tell how far there is to fall."

This is a gifted poet, for sure—one fully aware of the ability of image to carry the burden of language, except there's no burden here. Not at all. These poems are at best richly elegiac and nostalgic, but the good kind of nostalgia, the kind that reconnects us with nature, with kin, with all the dead poets and people in our lives.

I loved the poem "De Kooning in Court at Eighty-Five" because it signals the opening (if not ripening) of the poet's maturity and strength as we reach the middle-of-the-middle of this fine collection. By the time we arrive at the next-to-last poem in this collection, "The Farmer," and read "Tonight I picture him out in field, / dancing barefoot in the muck / and hollering, everything possible."

And everything *is*. Everything is recorded with great resonance in *As if Gravity Were a Theory*, a fine collection and a great opening of the human heart and spirit. I wish Don Colburn godspeed with his voice and poetry. He clearly has a bright future with his words with this talisman of a first book I will forever treasure because, though I did not find it, I can be its keeper . . . to share of it with you and with whomever else you care to gift it.

Salud & saludos,

Virgil Suàrez

There

Water, bone, bed, bedrock –
whatever is underneath, below what's below.
Sudden touchable quiet, shadow
of a shadow. Weather. Sadness turning
ordinary. Nameless illness coming on.
A knock at the door so gentle
it could be anything. Distance.
The just thing not said, or said too late
or said exactly and without mercy.
Wind rising. Whatever might rise.

Elegy in March

I thought of you this afternoon
as I bent down under the old front oak
to pick up sticks. They were all over –
twigs, branches, whole limbs broken off
under the wet heft of a late winter snow
and broken again against the ground
with their own weight crashing.
Scabbed, cindery, riddled by insects,
the windfall snapped easily in my hands,
all its give gone,
                                        and I gathered them,
thinking you would have too, and how to a child
this once seemed pointless,
like picking litter from a parking lot,
which you also insisted on. Now
six armloads of dead oak lie stacked
on the porch – enough to kindle
in the soft ash on cold stone
a month of fire.

Storm on Lopez Island

This must be what it looks like to drown,
the evergreens hurling and flailing,
raining cones. Everything gives up
an angled look of motion
or resistance, the ragged cliffs
and seaweedy rocks at the tideline,
summer-tall grasses that blaze and riffle
like fear along a deer's flank,

and to hear anything else –
the sea's repeating crash, or gulls,
the foghorn's warning over the far reef
or any voice, even my own –
I have to cock my head, one ear
into the gale, the other in the skull's lee.

Wrecking Ball

Passersby can't keep from watching
as it floats up, a two-ton teardrop
sky-tethered, and sways and swings

to kiss a brick wall plumb
to rubble. Suddenly the old hotel
is a cutaway, whole rooms

bashed open to available light
and dust that rises despite the firehose
arcing its water like white noise.

What's left becomes a monument,
ashen, the color of old ice,
oddly soft in the smoke-light.

Inside the swivel cockpit blazoned
Big Or Small We Ball Them All
a man in a yellow hardhat delicately

tugs on levers, and the ball keeps up
its assault and battery, its making room
for a parking lot. Another wall gives way,

bristling with rebar, and the ground
heaps up, a scree of brickbats, chunks
of plaster, pipe, viny wiring.

Obliteration can be beautiful
and talented, an art. The man
working the levers must believe that,

and a crowd has gathered on the sidewalk,
pausing at rush hour to stare wistfully
at ruin. They make bad jokes about Baghdad

and Beirut and the earthquake in Armenia,
then cheer each magnificent hit
as if it were a grand slam,

envying that man his work
so radical, so literal.

At Kennedy & Georgia

Each corner, people stand in the rain,
waiting for the bus, for the light to change,
a cab, a break in the rain.
We're all waiting in the rain.
The mom-and-pop waits with its
Cold Beer Wine Ice Refreshment
and across, Scipio the Florist
with *Wedding Arrangements On Short Notice.*
The Princess Salon of Beauty is waiting,
basement room to rent, and that empty house,
windows boarded, brick sprayed green.

Today, when every story begins with rain
and grows toward gray light, abstraction
seems unnecessarily abstract. The words
on the signs evaporate. Water. Wet. What?

Red, white and blue flags drip onto the lot
where used cars wait to be used.
An old woman with a red umbrella
tries the door of a Country Squire wagon,
looking for a dry place to smoke,
as a schoolbus slides by – in its rear window
a face with pigtails and huge eyes.
She smiles, waves.

Edward Dickinson, Emily's Dad

His effort at a smile in photographs
came out a lowering scowl –
thin lips, nosebeak, drill-bit eyes,
high collar like a brace.
And what could he make of her
upstairs with her quick pen: *too busy*
with his briefs to notice what we do.
And quicker still: *He never played.*

Lawyer, congressman, a diehard
Millard Fillmore Whig, trustee
at the local lunatic hospital,
pillar of the First Congregational
she never joined. Such fierce belief
in melioration (his word, and not
a word she'd lift her hat to) –
yet chary too, for God knew

where the written-down might lead:
He buys me many books,
but begs me not to read them...
Still, he loved fine horses
and grew passionate about winning
the railroad in from Belchertown.
Once he left his wife a note to say
how beautifully the new stove drew.

Everything in its place at the right time
was all he wanted, a rational happiness
which ruled out tantrums, glamour,
daydreams, poems. Emily again,
a letter to her brother:
We do not have much poetry,
father having made up his mind
that it's pretty much all real life...

Except the night he saw cold fire
across the northern sky
and ran to church to pull the bellropes,
wanting witnesses. Each livid streak
thriving in its unreal place –
aurora – and he knew:
no time for rational happiness,
no time for prose.

Motel, East Ohio

The woman behind the makeshift front desk,
who lives here with her kids, wants to know
if I've come for dog races or the jamboree
in Wheeling. Just the poetry festival, I say –
Did you ever know James Wright?
(A long shot.) No, she says,
but if he's a poet from around here
my mother must have known him.
She reaches into a steel drawer
and begins to read me poems her mother wrote,
like "Ode to a Hat":
Hat lying still on the bedroom chair,
I wonder why you were put there...
Which sounds stupid but it isn't.
It was her husband's hat, his way
of telling her something
and the poem her way of talking back.
This becomes important, to me I mean,
as I stand there holding my credit card.
Not the words exactly, their hurried sing-song,
but a daughter's need to hear them again
above the traffic.

Martins Ferry

If this were a letter to James Wright,
I would tell him how the rain colored everything
in its own image and how the road into town,
like the tracks and the river alongside,
is still the road out of town. I'd mention
they've renamed it for Lou "The Toe" Groza,
who made a living kicking for the Browns,
and how it still goes past the hobo jungle
and the dark red barns of Wheeling-Pittsburgh Steel,
how the bridge arcs its black latticework
above the river.

In the old high school auditorium –
hard seats, halflight, a purple curtain
hiding the basketball court –
the poets on stage are talking about rivers,
not just the Ohio a few streets east,
but all the rivers they have gathered at:
Monongahela, Delaware, Hudson, Iowa, Styx.
For they know a river leads back to the past
and down to the sea, all that lovely corruption
and a far shore.

Ten years,
and we're still dredging metaphor
out of that river. This morning's paper

hollers "RIVER YIELDS BOUND BODY"
above a gaudy photo of pink dogwood.
Yields, as if the Ohio gave it up,
the body a hostage or a harvest.
A barge worker found it upriver near the dam,
tied like a calf, waterlogged. No one knows.

From the high school steps you can still see
all the way to the river and Terminal Bridge
and downstream to the blue gap
where sky divides the hills, two states.
Even from here a river changes the world.
I want to tell James Wright
the Ohio's pretty much the same,
still on its way to Wheeling,
watering down what men do to it.
Tired, necessary beauty,
it keeps on toward us and away.

Differences

in memory of William Stafford

There was your knack for sounding regional
in every region and the way you swam out
past the single-minded, past the blocked on shore
belaboring their alibis. Such gumption

could hold a poet afloat in the cold sea
or start a car on ice,
the poems sifting down like snowflakes:
differences made of tiny differences.

I think of you in your brim hat,
white shirt and old jeans,
a morning's words in your shoulderbag,
crossing the grass to sit with us

in a circle outside the old Fort Worden
schoolhouse. It was the summer of '84
and I wanted to be your student. But you
were tricky like wind and nearly

drove me crazy when you refused,
coyote-faced, to praise or blame.
You wouldn't let us, any more than generals,
use your mind. You steered us back

toward recklessness and I've just begun
to understand this need to give a poem up
not to miss the next one.
No one had ever leaned on me

to lower my standards, make grammar
an enemy, greet failure gratefully.
All these heresies – a life – in harmony
under the voice. A poem finds its way

the way you'd listen as you roved a field
alone, alert for local differences.

What I Didn't Tell Stephen

When I tried to explain, Stephen said
no problem, he too was behind
after trips to St. Louis and Seattle,
and happy to shift the subject, I said
isn't Seattle beautiful –
and we joked stupidly about rain.
I asked if the mountains were out
and Stephen said oh sure, now and then
Rainier loomed up, an alabaster ghost.
Yet something made him uneasy,
maybe the work wouldn't
get done, one more espresso
or two and soon the morning turns
to afternoon. Typical East Coast attitude,
I thought, who grew up in Massachusetts
and moved to D.C. for the sake of a job –

and wasn't it green in the Northwest,
lush for late winter, mildly spectacular,
heather, broom, grass, moss,
everything growing like mad
and the horizon inviting you out
past doubt, past the past, and promising
blue lupine in the sun come midsummer,
not to mention the water everywhere,
snowmelt and runoff and rivers of fish,

the Sound, even the sea there is a sound,
asking you to come see
through the fine rain, come listen,
come sit and wait for an afternoon –
I didn't say this but I've been thinking
how I'd love to light out one morning
west all the way to the coast.

Ferry Crossing, With Lines from Arthur Dove

Blunt as a saucer, the *Klickitat*
arcs west by north across the tide,
trailing its wake through the chop.
A work of nature has no need
of things to lean upon for meaning,
the painter wrote. The pale volcano
grows impossibly with distance, floating
on mist of its own thawing,
while I scan the interval for something
to lean on. Crossing water is a glimpse
of what could deepen. The capable sky
lets down its midday blaze
evening will blow out candle by candle.
One shore falls away, another looms.
Is that the meaningless wind?
Or what feels like wind against our going?

As If Gravity Were a Theory

Bozeman Airport

Snow is falling everywhere, even
up from the tarmac in the trembling
around the engine barrels.
Two men in earmuffs in a cherry picker
aim pink foam from a fire hose;
the wing melts down to metal.
An inch from my nose the plexiglass
ticks and stipples into archipelagoes
of water. One of the men waves a broom
as if gravity were a theory
and we slide back, slow in the weather,
to turn. Runway lights like blue matchheads.
The sky kneels down. Bits of sleet
fly off the engines like sparks,
crazy in the winglights. Then a jerky hurtling,
faster, till the airfield gives way
to sheer air. Nothing outside
has a name, the Bridger Range invisible,
ranches big as counties – gone.
No cottonwoods to give the river away,
no river. No earth, no edge. Not one fact
to tell how far there is to fall.

Local News

Ten years after,
I remember two things:
It was a mild, cloudless afternoon
and the sick boy wore a wool cap
indoors, down to his eyes
which were not scared.
No. Three things. I was scared.

The Telling

Swannanoa, N.C.

Just enough snowfall to turn the ground
treacherous and bare trees beautiful,
the world going black-and-white,
stunned like a photograph.
A friend was dead at thirty.
I leaned against the shatterproof
glass to phone my wife.
"Paul's dead" is how I told her
because *died* was a lie
and I couldn't yet say *murdered*
or *stabbed.* Courage by degrees
in the telling, then nothing more to say,
so we said it over and over
and hung up dumb, winded.

Later, among strangers, I learned
to say it again and – *listen, Paul* –
people who never saw your face
saw something awful happening
in my face. I told them how exquisitely
picky you were, how time after time
you saved me from myself,
how outrage came over you quietly,
blushing when it counted –
and everything they will ever know of you
is what I whispered then.

Toward the End of the Year

Again

Sweet odor of leafrot
drifts up from the ground.
A frail chill flourishes
deep green in grass.
Another month, one
hard frost, and it will
burn down to pallor.
Again, a season of windfalls:
crabapples, cold rain.
Pin oak leaves, nearly the last,
spiral down cloudshadow –
upturned hands.

First Ice

Each year it surprises, the first
black ice of winter
brimming the pond – skim enough
to stand a gull. Sudden glass
traps silver pins of air
like nerves. A dry leaf
could slide forever there.

Ice too grows old,
outgrows itself, straining
till it shifts and cracks, skin
riddled by sun and snowdust.
But now it's new, and faultless,
clarity reaching into gaps
of rippling. Somewhere hidden
is the alchemy, the quick edge.

Afternoons

Skywritten season, days like milk.
Trees become their bones, linear
and stripped, unfit to shade
or shelter dwindling afternoons.
A few silhouetted nests, like clots,
ride the branching sky-shatter.
Coming east out of the mountains
the way the wind prevails
against the pastoral
was neither turning back
nor home, but yet another leaving.

First Snow

Thanksgiving morning, and my long skis
brush over in slow 4/4 –
phrew phrew phrew phrew –
but imagine the first cold-crazy time
ironclad rain turned feathery
and someone saw: rain that lasted,
glazing each body it touched,
even the drear air it fell through.
All the earth could do was wait
beneath the frozen burning.

Prayer

Habit's hold is so strong
that when I called long-distance
days after the death of my friend's son

he said How's it going?
and I said OK, how about you?
and he said Oh, up and down,

meaning this was the worst.
Then silence sounded
like the biggest room.

He was honest, my friend said,
really honest. At 22,
you could tell him anything

and he'd listen. People trusted him.
There must have been things
he couldn't talk about.

I've always thought belief
in God at such moments
is cheating, so I said Larry

maybe you should go
dig in the garden, split wood,
swim laps, take a long walk.

I wished for something
I could do. And Larry said
Pray, it's all we can.

II

Given

Whatever happened yesterday or just
now. Whatever light comes in
through my reflection. My next
thought as soon as it fastens,

these words after I erase them.
Happiness, when it comes, so sudden,
like a lucky stumble in talk.
Old news: starlight, thunder, rust.

A friend, the tumor cut out of her thigh,
trying to remember how it was
to dread something else.
Any pattern just before it ends,

then the lack of it.
My life every day becoming
what I have not done.

The Luxury of Distance

In spite of the news
and what the world chooses to tell itself,
death this week is not a brick wall,
not a bullet, a needle, a cliffleap
or quick implosion under the breastbone.
Death this week is nothing but a thin skin
a life leaks through quietly,
too slow to notice. Each day
a day seeps to the other side.
Each day but one, another waits.
Sometimes, with the luxury of distance,
you can feel it,
the strongest part of yourself.

Clouds and Circumstances

Circumstances are like clouds
continually gathering and bursting...
— John Keats

A man who coughs up blood
knows circumstance
and any Englishman knows clouds
so one who knew at 25 he'd die
at 25 must have seen them gathering,
ready to burst. Clouds change
the feel of the touching world.
They float or glint or thunder in
and make you think: *autumnal*,
winter coming and – oh, spare me
all that vain philosophy.
A cloud's a cloud – moisture.
One version of sky.

Yesterday the clouds were puffy-edged
and beautiful, so far apart they couldn't
interrupt the sun that lit their fringes
and brightened all of downtown,
high-rise towers, bus lanes, ginkgos
and the flurrying golden locust leaves.
But the uppity volcano on TV
had a satin cap, lenticular
and glistening, an omen for today
which came up circumstantial, almost

Keatsian – *no, don't* –
a morning chill that afternoon won't
rid itself of. Sky lowering a hundred
shades of gray. Promising to rain.

To The Computer Who Lost to a Human at Chess

Chess is wider than logic.
— Garry Kasparov

People gloried in your slow defeat
mistaken for fate. Mind over matter!
The old ache for allegory. But look:
The machine never gave in. Logically,
the game was over by the seventeenth move,
when (playing black) you had to sacrifice
your queen. Ah, but *sacrifice* is a word
even smart computers haven't learned
and play dragged on and on,
Kasparov toying, your software
sifting 700,000 trees a second
and still missing the woods.

You never flinched, not even
an actuary's wince at the logical
loss of a queen. Grief, empathy –
not your strongpoints. A silicon chip
can't outwit the champ this century,
Kasparov brags, but he knows
one day you'll know by heart
a million million moves, if not
something wider – grief, say,
or hope, and when hope is gone,
how much like sacrifice it is to play on.

Ode to "Launch"

before a class on Launching Poems

A rowboat, maybe, or a bottlerocket,
even a crusade. If you're Zeus,
a thunderbolt. Helen's face, a thousand
battleships. Or on the news
a politician with his five-point plan.
But a few words promising
more than what they're made of?

Not quite the same as thrust,
fling, heave, hurl, get
the show on the road. Not pretty
like *cholesterol*, or funny like
banana. One click from *lunch*
or *raunch* or the dark stain
of that American terror and its mob.

Admen can bubblewrap it
into a noun, but in the imagination –
all verb. Stare long enough
and it will lift off. A word
who's been with other words – ideal
for starters. Any moment
it might just go someplace.

To Bill Buckner on his Release by the Red Sox

The papers total your career
in easy symmetry: 2,000-plus
big league hits and one
stupendous World Series bungle.
Fate's a bad hop, Billy Buck,
or no hop at all. We had to watch
nothing change on the TV replay.
You were shading Mookie perfectly,
though I bet some nights sleep would come easier
if you'd been hopelessly out of range.

OK, maybe Stanley wouldn't have
gotten to the bag in time.
Knowing this you know nothing
except what makes a life look back.
One stupid grounder (that replay in the mind) –
enough to justify ten thousand coaches shouting
ten million times: *Eye on the ball!*
How many times can you wrap your ankles in ice
and Ace bandages and lace those ridiculous high-tops
to your rickety shins? In a week, Buck,

I'm forty, and you're a lousy reminder
of how young thirty-seven is.
Sure, you can still get around

on a fastball, foul off junk from the corners
and slap any fat-hanging curve into the gap.
But even designated hitters have to
get down the line, Buck.
You're a jalopy with bad wheels.
You're the only ballplayer I ever saw
run with his arms. I remember

how you scored from second in the fifth game
on Dewey's hit and made it look incredibly
difficult – windmilling around third,
bowlegged and flatfooted, shimmying
till you flopped and skidded home.
NBC loved it and so did we each time
the replay took forever. But that was before
the ground ball and the blank ending,
early winter and its unredeeming spring, and now –
getting cut midseason, a thing they call release.

The Art of Poetry

Of course it came out short
of what the body wants.
Enough, I said, slapping
my knees. What's the use? Why
waste time, your only life,
turning yourself crazy?
You could be fixing lunch,
running a wash, clipping
your nails or the lawn, some
task with a beginning
and an end so you know
where to start over. Weeds,
laundry, hunger – no lack
of fresh material.
But silence grows back too,
out of the feeling that
couldn't contain it. The
wrong words are another
way to begin. Enough,
I said. And sat back down.

In the Workshop After I Read My Poem Aloud

All at once everyone in the room says
nothing. They continue doing this and I begin to know
it is not because they are dumb. Finally

the guy from the Bay Area who wears his chapbook
on his sleeve says he likes the poem a lot
but can't really say why and silence

starts all over until someone says she only has
a couple of teeny suggestions such as taking out
the first three stanzas along with

all modifiers except "slippery" and "delicious"
in the remaining four lines. A guy who
hasn't said a word in three days says

he too likes the poem but wonders why
it was written and since I don't know either
and don't even know if I should

I'm grateful there's a rule
I can't say anything now. Somebody
I think it's the shrink from Seattle

says the emotion is not earned and I wonder
when is it ever. The woman on my left

who just had a prose poem in *Green Thumbs & Geoducks*

says the opening stanza is unbelievable
and vindication comes for a sweet moment
until I realize she means unbelievable.

But I have my defenders too and the MFA from Iowa
the one who thinks the *you* is an *I*
and the *they* a *we* and the *then* a *now*

wants to praise the way the essential nihilism
of the poem's occasion serves to undermine
the formality of its diction. Just like your comment

I say to myself. Another admires the zenlike polarity
of the final image despite the mildly bathetic
symbolism of sheep droppings and he loves how

the three clichés in the penultimate stanza
are rescued by the brazen self-exploiting risk.
The teacher asks what about the last line

and the guy with the chapbook volunteers it suits
the poem's unambitious purpose though he has to admit
it could have been worded somewhat differently.

Why Sarah Will Never Suffer Writer's Block

We ordered a medium – half pepper and onion,
half plain, no mushrooms, no meat –
and waited for our number to be called.
I was wishing it could all be so simple
and grumbling how badly the morning had gone,
how hard to get started.
Then Sarah, who's eight, said OK,
here's what you do, go look
in a book, find a topic you like
and whatever it is, make up a rhyme –
like you could go

the blue whale

has a slippery tail...

She shrugged, rolled her quibble-proof eyes
and turned her hands inside out: See?
Now it was my turn to shrug and our number
came up, but Sarah kept on:
You know – the biggest animal on earth?
But you could pick Halloween or jelly beans
or a ghost. It could be anything.

De Kooning in Court at Eighty-Five

Still able to brush his teeth
if handed a toothbrush,
so why not a paintbrush? Why not
an island of performance (the technical term)
in the midst of suffering, his loss
of the part of a mind we see the loss of
first, which may or may not hurt
the part that paints in silence,
no longer listening to Mozart
or any visitors. They see canvases
he neither signs nor sells
but simply paints, throwing
his whole frail body into it, color
flowing from his fingertips.

His daughter's lawyer wants him called
incompetent, with round-the-clock nurses
and studio time through the roof.
Yet he paints away each morning,
masterfully, they say, *and still evolving.*
A doctor guesses he's in the sixth stage,
the seventh being final. His guardian,
court-appointed, says he won't talk back –
works *all the time inside himself.*

Gazing out, can he see them

dickering over his pictures?
Dealers are calling him a great property,
by which they mean praise,
for they are eager to have him:
the work – brilliant, abstract –
the part of him that speaks.

Etheridge

July. Port Townsend. Early afternoon
and already you were pathetic, fingers
around the neck of a brown sack
under the trees, words botched and rambling.
And that evening, after we'd waited so long
in the dark of the theater
for the only black man in town,
when you came on stage,
brushed aside the mike and opened your throat
to *Willow, Weep for Me*, slow and deep, wavering –
I cringed. But then you turned to poems –
belly songs made up in the joint, about Slick
and Hard Rock and Malcolm and Mr. K
the Love of My Life, and said them by heart
in perfect pitch, never missing a syllable.
Next morning, catching you
weaving across the grass, as barn swallows
flew sheer in the sun, I thought perhaps
you'd climb into the light again to sing.

To a Condemned Man Now Dead

Not that you were too young to die,
though thirty-five is too young, and not because
they killed you in the middle of the night
the most premeditated way. Not exactly
that you didn't deserve it, either,
having shot an old man for his rare coins
and killed another for cash whose sister-in-law
was not all right in the head but knew to scream
until you silenced her forever.
And not because their friends and next-of-kin
stood by the road, waiting to whoop it up
when the hearse slid by, or because Mr. Sellers,
whose wife you kidnapped from the jiffy store
and raped and shot, was there at midnight
to watch them tuck down the blindfold
and buckle you in. And surely
not because you said, "I'm sorry,"
and dragged God into that thick room –
"whatever the Lord sees fit" – to take you home.
"Too easy," muttered Sellers,
who watched you twitch and jerk.
But to know so well what killing is
and call it mercy –
nothing in this life is easy to believe.

Late

for my brother

I knew the reason would outgrow
the tremor in your voice.
It grew to this: A boy, your student,
died last night. "We tried to save him,
but it was too late," you said.
"He hung himself."

After a moment's thought
that what you meant was "hanged,"
I nudged you on toward vagueness from the fact –
autumn's rainy progress, football scores.
My questions were like props,
as if it mattered where the boy was from,

the boy who died,
whose heart you tried to be,
the boy whose ribs you cracked
to inspire the useless blood,
whose death you chased
for near an hour.

I didn't ask you
how you knew to stop
and did you cry
and did you feel like God
and do you wonder if that dying boy
was glad you failed?

To Lee Atwater on his Fortieth Birthday

Now that you've stripped the bark off that little bastard Dukakis
  and made Willie Horton his running mate,
Now that your landslide is old news,
Now that you've cut your own blues album with B.B. King,
Now that the Grand Old Party has kicked you upstairs,
Now that mid-speech your left foot started to twitch,
Now that they've stuck 10 radioactive needles into your brain,
Now that it hasn't worked,
Now that the X-rays show a second shadow blooming,
Now that acupuncture and red underwear and steroids haven't
  worked,
Now that dream therapy and laughter, The Three Stooges on video
  haven't worked,
Now that nothing has worked,
Now that your boy-face is bloodshot and bloated,
Now that old friends don't know you,
Now that your bowels shut down and your left arm dangles,
Now that your baby daughter is not safe on your lap,
Now that you've added a fourth (the Bible) to your favorites Plato
  and Sun Tzu and Macchiavelli,
Now that you dare to ask God for patience and white blood cells,
Now that you've told Life magazine,
Now that you've told your sick father you loved him,
Now that you've told the truth like a man, and like a woman,
Cruelty has bared to you its cruel side.

Election Day Omens

It's raining in Cleveland, and snow fell all night
across the Texas Panhandle. A low disturbance
builds over the northern Plains.

The Ukrainian vote last weekend ended
in a dead heat. A man running for president
of Uruguay promised to focus on local issues.

The Norway maples on 21st are more vivid
than ever. Rain brings out the orange
much as sunshine does. This is not ironic.

"Sic Semper Tyrannis!" shouted John Wilkes Booth
as he leaped from the president's bloody box
at Ford's. He'd been on stage before

in tragedies, a profile in the paper says.
"Don't let us be sad," he also said.
"Life is short – and the world is beautiful."

Yaw is 6 years old and rides the bus to school.
He got his name in Ghana. Dinosaurs aren't real,
Yaw says, but they have a lot of bones.

"President Garfield's Hornpipe"
is in the wrong key and hard to play

on a pennywhistle. Unlike "The Pope's Toe."

A lady in a downpour at Fremont and 15th
holds a sign: *Honk If You Voted Blue.*
No way – until the pickup cuts me off.

Don't taunt the alligator till you cross the creek,
says CBS's talking head, meaning the polls
in Ohio haven't closed. It's raining in Cleveland.

On the Eighteenth Day of Bombing, I Go for a Hike

Midwinter you can see past the trees,
white oaks and tulip poplars, tops golden
in the low sun. Today, not a cloud.
The old fire road leads up Old Raggedy,
up to boulders and the sheer outcrop
silver with snowmelt. What matters lasts:
rock, timber, streambeds with predicaments
where the water falls. But also that man
resting with his boy at the roadedge.
He is sweating, half out of breath.
A plastic bottle dangles off his pack.
"Left a piece of my mind up top," he says,
but I don't hear him right. I hear "peace of mind."
The blue air opens. He tries again.
"I nailed Saddam's mug to the wall of the lean-to
and wrote *Hit me with your best shot.*"
I look at the boy of maybe ten
who looks at the ground and shifts his pack.
The plummeting infallible creek
finds the bottom of the hollow,
where hemlocks darken white water.
We stand quiet in the fire road, justifying
what isn't said. What is said is
"How was it up on the mountain?"
And the boy: "Pretty cold. We nearly froze.
But you should have seen the stars."

Veterans Day Night at the War Memorial

All along the glassy black wide angle
they look away and back. Some carry
candles or white carnations. A woman
reaches to graverub a block from '67
onto a page of her brochure;
it prints like a darkroom photograph.
Odd how we abstract a thing – a war –
to make it real, a wall of losses.
Down the slow line I find myself
staring at a man ambushed by a name.
He's in old boots and fatigues,
cap in his hands – balding, paunchy,
grizzle-cheeked, about my age.
He can't stop looking down
at his boots, the litter of medals,
can't stop sobbing in bursts, his face
clenching and unclenching like a fist
or a heart. I might have been that man
or either of us become a chiseled stone.
Years ago I came to this mall
to march with thousands,
easy as it was to leave the war
to strangers such as these –
the one here now, and one
he sees and doesn't see.

The Slave Station at Gorée Island, Senegal

In the postcard, the sun is shining,
as it shone then. The walled yard
is empty and bright, a double staircase
curves in a horseshoe to the balcony.
Way in back, a tiny oblong of blue
shimmers where the tunnel leads to the sea.
Left and right are the stone cells
where they lay in the dark by the hundreds
until a ship came and they were taken for weighing.
More than 60 kilos, a male was man enough
to be sold for a barrel of rum.
Buyer and seller stood in the shade
on the balcony, pricing the ones on the steps,
a female by her age and her breasts,
the sex the traders had with her, children
by their teeth. The ship was waiting
with a wooden gangplank they walked out on,
over the water, chained to each other.

The Hill

Out along the slippery clay path
to the brook of dry stones and over
the humped wooden footbridge,
past sumac, sycamore, coils of bittersweet
and the frost-burned meadow, to the hill –
it had been years. The gray bulk of her coat
leaned into the hill,
in her feet a fine urgency.

Halfway, something thrilled in her chest –
her legs halted and she took back air.
Everything for a moment was new
and near. Then it was mere pain
giving way to an ache, something she knew,
and she straightened against the dull
wavy relief of her life, cold fingers
tucking the little white pill
under the curl of her tongue.

The purse snapped shut –
a sound so ordinary she started,
and felt the difference of a door closed.
She looked out over the pale grass,
the bittersweet and the stone-dry brook,
and turning away from the hill,
she walked back down.

4 Orange

at Children's Hospital

A skittery streak of darkness marks
where they split his chest and pried open.
Just like open heart, says his father, proud.
It was his teenaged right lung, three spots.
First time, they took ten inches out of his arm
plus a hunk of shoulder. Now he sits up
in pajama bottoms and a baseball cap,
Hank Jr. singing somewhere in the room,
and talks of getting back to roof work,
marrying Angel when she's through school.
It only hurts to roll over or cough
or breathe deep, so on the way to X-ray
he lingers in the rainbow-painted rec room
to shoot a rack of pool with his bad arm
dangling. Still swears he'll drive home tomorrow,
eight hours, counting stops. *Then what?*
He shrugs and leans over to spit
bits of Skoal into a white cup.
Back home, rock maple and Virginia creeper
are full of blazes, the father says.
And then? And then it could be rough,
says the old man, his son out of the room.
This operation, see, it depends on his life.

Cul-de-sac

The first transparent air in months,
Labor Day sun throwing clear
shadows – and here in the northern South,
openness, windows flung wide.
At dusk, cicadas friz the tree-dark
to a sweet sheeny pulsing.

Yesterday, in a cul-de-sac,
a trash truck backed up
slowly over a two-year-old.
A neighbor saw it happening and tried
to snatch her out of the way, but the girl
stumbled playfully backwards laughing.

What is clarity and sweetness to them now?
Parents who picked a safe street for their daughter,
neighbor who lunged a moment late,
the child who played along.
And the driver – the one off to the left,
the sunlit one, his head in his hands.

Days

Days he railed against the blank
wall of dailiness, shaking his fist, moving
huge invisible clouds across the sky.
Then in an instant, for nothing he had done,
the air burned clean and the wall sang back
a concert of stones placed carefully
one against another. He was delivered
from a day's work to a day's work,
happiness, sorrow, almost in unison,
all part of what he wanted. Some days
the light hurt too much to swallow.

Not Another World

letter from the artists colony

My very own cabin in the woods
has one room and a broom
and a brown bear on its hind legs
dancing with a fish on the piano.
My cabin has a wicker rocker by the fire,
an army cot in one corner and
bolted where I can reach it easily
from sleep – a pencil sharpener.
There's heat and a hotpot and nine
yard-sale lamps. No one to talk to
or talk back, just a few good books
I probably won't read.

I get here walking
a dirt road you could get lost on.
It's late September and the hardwoods
are turning, geese going over.
Mornings I see breath. White birches
show the pines how to stand out in woods.
The stars are amazing, like stars.

The road to my cabin is dirt
but leads both ways. The windows
on all sides look out, and in.
There are ghosts on the walls, with names.
Wind in the trees came from somewhere

and just now a tractor-trailer
downshifted on the two-lane the woods
keep out of sight. Even that loner
Thoreau walked back into town
from his shack and his rows of beans
and tinkered with his diary
when he wrote the book. The road
to my cabin leads both ways.
It is not my road, nor my cabin.

Only Life

for Victor Cohn

It's only life, my friend would say
when everydayness leaned in
on him. I knew not to take him lightly,
for Vic was older and had been to war,
had lost a job or two, a wife,
his shirt in the market.
Plus, Vic is from Minneapolis
and rarely overstates things. Not bad, he said
when Jack Morris pitched 10 shutout innings
in the seventh game of the World Series
or spring showed up with daffodils
after a week of cold rain.
For years, I knew exactly what
Vic was saying about his life
and mine: no biggie, suck it up, don't think
so much about your own stubbed toe.
Until today, when we met for lunch
at the Chinese place in Vic's high-rise
so he wouldn't have to walk outside.
First time I'd seen him since the biopsy
and the start of what's left.
Vic was wearing an old Twins ballcap,
not wanting to scare me. We hugged
clumsily and sat. You know what Adam said
to Eve in the Garden, he deadpanned,

and I laughed at his punch line, same
as in the old days. We ordered egg rolls,
asparagus and sweet-and-sour shrimp,
with chopsticks and tea. Like before.
Then, mid-sentence, Vic's voice
gave out and he held up one hand
to say don't worry, this won't be pretty
but give me a moment – and coughed
from way down, a slurry ruckus.
He gathered himself to finish
his thought, then caught a breath.
It's only life, I blurted,
hating what I had just said,
except Vic raised his index finger
and smiled and nodded: *But life.*

III

Persona

You again? Look,
you're not the only one
who woke up wanting better lines.
I'm late for my day job,
plus I'm due to read at group tonight
and we talked last time about the need
to stop saying I – or should it be *me*? –
so much. This is where
you come in. Yes, you – over there,
skulking in the shadows, so quiet
you could be a pronoun or an understudy
for you know who. Right now, though,

the stage is yours, you're on
your own, whatever song and dance
you sing and dance is yours.
Don't be afraid to ad lib –
part of the deal. Whoops, watch out
for the stage lights that blind you
to the few folks out there.
They won't know it's you,
or if they do, it won't be you
they blame. And that red felt hat
with the peacock feather, slightly
askew, suits you fine.

Last Day of Summer, 1954

Morning came up dark, a clanging
gutterspout, my window shut
by someone in the night. And wind –
a locomotive dragging thunder
down the strange, endangered sky.

I was too young to be afraid
or useful like my brother.
He fiddled with cordless radios
to track the atmosphere's collapse.
Dad was somewhere else. Mother worried,
lit candles and buttered cold biscuits
while, huge and reckless in the trees,
the air worked round against itself,
this *Carol.* Not the name of a girl
but wilder – noondusk, cloudroar –

and when the gusts had spun their way to sea,
afternoon hung warm and humid as breath,
sweet with sap. The ground was gone,
a thrash of branches and the pale veiny
undersides of leaves, two maples fallen
across each other.

I climbed down one,

shinnied out along the bark
to where the trunk split off,
the fresh white splintered glistening.

Birds

Not just the cardinal blood-bright
against the snow, but juncos, jays,
starlings dark on a wire,
and not just the way they hold me still
by the grace of accuracy, fly exactly
to a halt and eat with their whole bodies.
Catbird, cowbird, oafish crows,
the heart-faced barn owl I never saw,
anonymous sparrows littering the yard –
I welcome them all,

like Mandelstam,
who had larger things to worry about.
Sparrows flew into his poems,
and orioles, like vowels. A goldfinch
could make him happy who always knew
he'd be arrested soon,
hard labor in a far cold place,
new poems still ringing in his ears,
the old ones stashed in cookpots.

Or like my mother, years ago, the time coming
when the man she loved who also loved birds
wouldn't leave the house each morning
for the train. Days – would they be
one rose-breasted grosbeak after another?

Lunch on the Way Home from Children's

When our charburgers didn't come,
Becca set the book of matches down exactly
for kickoff and taught me the waiting game.
Finger off thumb, one flick, and the matchbook
slid spinning across the dark shellac
into my lap. I sent it skidding back,
dared it to hang off the edge just short
of plunging over. Isn't that the goal
even when you're not sixteen?
If any part of the matchbook stuck out
past the rim – touchdown, six points.
Sometimes she'd shake salt
to slicken the field, make things more
dicey. No matter where my shot landed,
Becca laughed as if she could forget
the MRI and what was growing.
Losing 12 to 6, I plucked
an ice cube from my glass
and flicked and she cried "Whoa-ho!"
as it sailed unstoppable over the edge.
I still see the love of mischief
in those eyes, so close to happy.

Morning Song

Day breaks open artlessly
across a field of switchgrass tossing
wild and easy in the windswell.
The weedy fastness gives way to a widening
brim of eastlight blazing the mist.
Spring is the dangerous season, awakening
this bee-crazed meadow to overgrowing –
and in me awe, and ache, avid to begin
like birds and the earth all over.

How to Say *Kwakiutl*

Imagine a grizzly bear
with frogs in its ears and a raven
perched on its head. It helps
to have watched a great heron
at the ragged edge of the sea

before it flaps and somehow
lifts off. Or if, in the dark,
you can make out a yellow cedar
bending to the water – maybe.
Like the wind, the rain, the rings

in the treetrunk the great bear
was carved from, or a sound
you hear for the first time, so old
you know it tells more than one
story: *Quawquawkeewogwah.*

No use squinting at the scant
letters or sounding them out.
Listen to one who hears his name
without looking. Close your eyes.
Say what he knew by heart.

In Cougar Country

after a warning by the Dosewallips ranger

1.

Go in small groups
and make enough noise
to keep from surprising
yourselves. Pepper spray
would have been a good idea.

2.

Stay calm and don't
run. Face the animal, stand
upright. Speak firmly
and give it at least one
way to escape.

3.

Do everything you can
to appear larger.

4.

Become more assertive.
Shout loudly, throw rocks.
Throw whatever you can find
without crouching down
or turning away.

5.

Fight back.
Keep your feet
or try to get up.
Whatever is left
to try, try.

Fall Migration at Brigantine

Instinct is just a word for comings and goings
we can't explain. November brings snow geese
to where the Jersey shore begins or ends,
this unison of marshgrass and mudflats.
And we too have come, a busful
up from the Smithsonian
in boots, plaid hats and binoculars,
our own brand of protective coloration,
eager for a peek at a green-winged teal
among the pintails, or a great blue
fishing from his standstill in the shallows.

We hadn't driven two blocks when someone
checked off *rock dove* and *ring-billed gull.*
Now a coot stalks the mudbank on galoshy feet
while redtails and turkey vultures
kettle high and slow along the thermals.
Across the bay the casino skyline rises
bluish in the haze. There are thresholds
everywhere but no clear lines:
land and water, fresh and salt, wilderness
and honkytonk. A season, this,

for crossing-over. Tundra swans come
and snow geese by thousands down from the Arctic
turn mudflats to a white shimmer. Look!

Another flock, high enough for twilight,
glittery wingbeats trembling the dark sky,
willed south by wind, shoreline, loss of light,
ancient pulls we nearly remember –
we who have gathered to watch
and call them by name.

The Moose

at MacDowell

No jokes, please, about a barn door
or the mouse-eared bat who sees
by how a sound comes back
(and does quite well, considering the dark)

but a moose and I
stood in the sun this morning
in that field
and whether he saw me I cannot say.

What luck, to happen along
right then, binoculars in hand,
for there he was – magnificent –
his muzzle trumpeting broad day.

Except, and here's the gist, I missed it.
The first in fifty years! exclaimed Louise,
who watched us from her breakfast table
and marveled how I dared so near.

The close-up moose I didn't see today
had knobby knees, a ragged goatee,
a hump in his back and a huge rack.
How many points? It's hard to know.

The moose I almost stumbled on
had fine Nixonian jowls and lonely eyes
and overall a slightly foolish look
you might not notice far away.

But may I say, I got distracted by a bird
that flew up from the corner of my eye –
distracted from that, oh, maybe
nine-hundred-pound hoofed beast

by a flitting warbler I lost in the sun
and a backlit tree. And a clump of ferns
going green to gold, they were lovely....
While he –

he sauntered plainly on, unfazed,
and grazed and paused and raised
his splendidly unwieldy head
in case someone was looking.

Emerson and I Stare at the Sunset

Saffron flaring from below,
beyond the land, never exactly ends
but where the mind wants a boundary,
gives over, infinite, to a blue
unison of ice and fire.
One star quickening and a new moon
cool as flutesong.
The only earth-caught thing:
a whittling of fir trees
lit black.

I am nothing. I see all,
says the transcendentalist –
his wide-eyed way of bracketing
the world. And I with my doubts
squint at the clarifying dusk,
the heaven becoming nothing
like itself, evening.
Evening. Evening till
I cannot disbelieve my eyes.

Touchstones

Cold and glossy with seawater,
they tarnish quickly in my hand,
so I fling them back under the waves.

Would the world sing if I let it be
and listened? If, wandering a new shore,
memory fell behind and I heard nothing
but this accumulating commonplace

of song? Though surely the wind
would have its say, whose roughening touch
the sunken stones will not be troubled by.

Sestina Insomnia

And here's the rub: It makes no sense,
the body treating its own want like dirt,
a field so beaten down by drought that rain
when it comes can't lose itself and travel
down to withered roots. Three sheep on a bicycle
built for two stand better odds than lying still

for this, these manic hours, on a still
hunt for sleep. You get the viral sense
you'll no more shake it than how to ride a bicycle.
Or say a runner thrown out at the plate kicks dirt
in the umpire's face. The ump, who longs to travel
the world, is stuck at home in the rain.

He knows one side will blame him for the rain.
Tell the mind not to think and the mind, still
at work, thinks *Why not?* It too loves travel
and unlike the umpire, needn't leave home. No sense
of place, promiscuous, the air fares dirt
cheap. My friend who rides his beat-up bicycle

ten miles to work each day says on a bicycle
you rediscover the world (including rain),
you're one with the road, blacktop or dirt,
the mind shuts down, goes blank, and still

leaves the body awake, each avid sense
thrilled with its part. No better way to travel,

he claims, yet sleep just now is a form of travel
beyond any spaceship, let alone a bicycle.
And who wants to merge with a road? Nonsense,
I would tell my friend. I love what rain
does to the earth without trying, but I still
feel no desire to watch it wash dirt

to mud. The ump calls "Strike!" on a curve in the dirt
and the crowd boos. He daydreams of travel
or falling asleep. The trick is to hold still
with the mind reaching out like spokes of a bicycle
wheel, radiant as daisies or June rain.
To see a star, look away. That makes sense

once it works, like a still-life or bicycle
gears. To the iron dirt, sleep is a softening rain.
It must enter softly, travel down far past sense.

Sunday Morning, Long-term Care Wing

The whole hillside stares back,
rain-bright green of the pines and grass,
and hardwoods coming late into spring,
bark glistening black.
Now a plume of white floats up,
lengthening in the updraft like smoke, or silk,
or breath. When it thins to fitful vanishing,
the green hill reasserts itself and the glass
half-reflects the long pastel walls
broken into doorways. Nothing, not even
another burst of boiler-wasted steam,
disturbs the glycerin air.

Pansies at the Modern

In the almost-quiet of the sculpture garden
their blooming carries
like song across flat water.
Then a different kind of unison:
five white birches, not quite straight,
with scars in the bark like Morse code.
They branch and taper toward the city
in new-delicate green.
But it is the blue beneath the trees
that changes everything – the old man
on a stone bench reading the News,
the fountain with its pool of wishes,
the disappointing clouds. Even Picasso's
heavy-bellied she-goat gazing there.

The Wish

for El

As heartache can go, ours wasn't much –
one yes we wanted more than we knew.
Now we've carried that silent longing
into the woods, switchbacking slow
across the shadows of hemlocks,
away from the shushing, silt-green North Fork
and up through the blowdown to these open meadows.

Does anyone believe all that happens
happens for the best? I know this:
A wish is never wrong.
A yellow monkeyflower has bloomed
among the mossy rocks by a runnel of snowmelt
and makes me glad – the extravagance,
how little depends on it.

Timberline

Where it had been dark enough for stars, for sleep,
a cry of light fell across the tent.
I stumbled out barefoot,
blind, half-dreaming catastrophe
and searchlights, a quarrel at least.
But it was a kind of lunacy
turning to luck. Bright chaos
dwindled to a nickel in the sky,
then grew back full as the mind's eye
rising with its cool unoriginal light.
I rested a long, silvery time,
slumped on a rock,
letting go of fear like breath.

The Farmer

for Ward Sinclair (1933-1995)

I've come in now out of the urban rain,
after a long run through the park
along the horse trail slick with mud.
The cloudfall caught me halfway around,
as far from home turning back as going on.
No thunder, no lightning, just the gray
sheen of rain hushing the woods
and reminding me of my friend
who threw off his desk job in the city
for a truck farm. We envied him
and rose from our desks to tell him
when he drove downtown, flatbed loaded
with squash, melons, baskets of beans,
whatever the earth gave back.
But when he shook his head low at the sun
and muttered, "Don't know what we're gonna do –
half an inch of rain since the first of May,"
I knew he really didn't know.
Tonight I picture him out in a field,
dancing barefoot in the muck
and hollering, everything possible.

Wildflowers

Until I heard the names in my own voice
I never saw them whole: chickweed, toothwort,
May apple, Dutchman's breeches, Indian pipe.
A list was my father's way of witnessing;
it made a flower real. And this afternoon
in the weedy meadow by the towpath,
I'm jotting odd names on a scrap of paper
for no one in particular, myself maybe
or my father. Back then I let him teach me
to look down at the ground for stars,
bells, shades of blue. He was never happier
than when we looked up accuracy's myriad names
and he wrote them out in slanted letters.
Now, over and over, like a child,
I say *gill-over-the-ground, gill-*
over-the-ground, gill-over-the-ground,
and in the saying see it blossom again
inside its spilled blue name.

Table of Contents